How Much Can a Bare Bear Bear?

What Are Homonyms and Homophones?

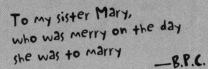

To my sister Mary,
who was merry on the day
she was to marry

—B.P.C.

Homonyms:

Two or more words that are pronounced the same and spelled the same but have different meanings

Homophones:

Two or more words that are pronounced the same but have different spellings and different meanings

How Much Can a Bare Bear Bear?

What Are Homonyms and Homophones?

by Brian P. Cleary

illustrated by Brian Gable

SCHOLASTIC INC.

New York Toronto London Auckland Sydney
Mexico City New Delhi Hong Kong Buenos Aires

Homonyms

are words that sound
and also look alike.

But they have
different meanings, as in
"Can you pass that can, Mike?"

Or "May I sail with you in May and coast all along the coast?"

These words are a blast
if you say them quite fast,

A **light** may be **light**,
like a small paper kite.

A **trunk** can be found
in a **trunk**.

But punch cannot punch, and at breakfast or lunch,

your jam cannot jam on a trumpet.

Now, some words sound identical but are spelled in different ways. These words are known as **homophones**,

like
praise

Though **homophones** have matching sounds, **their** meanings aren't the same.

And there isn't any question,
they're as fun as any game.

A horse can get hoarse from talking, of course.

A ewe could take you on a stroll.

A fowl can be foul.
A toad can be towed.

An heir mustn't err in the air.

A Whale can Wail.

A male can mail.
A pair might just
pare a big pear.

A bust can be bused
by a driver you trust,

and Barry
can bury
a berry.

A band could be banned
if they get out of hand,

and Mary (who's merry)
can marry.

But the sea cannot see,
and it's clear as can be
that a ball will not bawl when it's rolled.

A moose has no use
for a bottle of mousse,
and a creek doesn't creak
when it's old.

But a bear
should be bare,

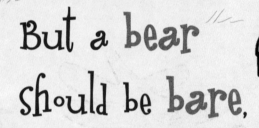

and it
wouldn't be rare
if Wood Would
be kept in a shed.

A Sioux
might not sue
if he knew
that the gnu that he bought
wasn't new like you said.

My niece could see Grease
both in Greece and in Nice.

A Czech could be
writing a
check.

A maid could be made
to be very afraid
when she heard
a big herd on the deck.

You could search the whole world,

While it spun and it whirled,

in each inn
and beneath every stone.

And you'd find no more pleasures than these great verbal treasures —

the **homonym** and **homophone!**

So, what are **homonyms** and **homophones**?

Do you know?

ABOUT THE AUTHOR & ILLUSTRATOR

BRIAN P. CLEARY is the author of the Words Are CATegorical™ series, including <u>A Mink, a Fink, a Skating Rink: What Is a Noun?</u> and <u>Hairy, Scary, Ordinary: What Is an Adjective?</u>, and of <u>Rainbow Soup: Adventures in Poetry</u>. He lives in Cleveland, Ohio.

BRIAN GABLE is the illustrator of <u>Under, Over, By the Clover: What Is a Preposition?</u>, <u>Pitch and Throw, Grasp and Know: What Is a Synonym?</u>, and the Make Me Laugh joke books. He lives in Toronto, Ontario, with his wife and two children.

ISBN-13: 978-0-439-93523-4
ISBN-10: 0-439-93523-7

12 11 10 9 8 7 6 5 4 3 2   6 7 8 9 10 11/0

Printed in the U.S.A.

First Scholastic printing, November 2006

23